Spectral Realms

No. 7 ‡ Summer 2017

Edited by S. T. Joshi

The spectral realms that thou canst see
With eyes veil'd from the world and me.

H. P. LOVECRAFT, "To a Dreamer"

SPECTRAL REALMS is published twice a year by Hippocampus Press,
P.O. Box 641, New York, NY 10156 (www.hippocampuspress.com).
Copyright © 2017 by Hippocampus Press.
All works are copyright © 2017 by their respective authors.
Cover art "The Game is Done!" by Gustave Doré (1832–1883) from
The Rime of the Ancient Mariner by S. T. Coleridge.
Cover design by Barbara Briggs Silbert.
Hippocampus Press logo by Anastasia Damianakos.

ISBN: 978-1-61498-204-3   ISSN 2333-4215

Contents

Poems

This Mountain of Skulls:

A Song to Sing in Hell

John Shirley

Charioteers,
rolling over the hills,
never did see
all the blood they spilled;
how it caught the moonlight,
which drew it like dew:
a secret essence
to the hungry moon.

And we never will climb
this mountain of skulls—
though we march to the heights
and we plod with these fools . . .
No, we never will climb
this mountain of skulls;
this pinnacle created
by the guns of the cruel.

There's a man in the Rockies
in a trailer of steel;
he gets drunk on red sake;
he wears blue spike heels.
Beneath a dozen graves
unmarked in the pines,
the souls of his slaves

discourse on his crimes.
And he'll never be caught
nor will justice be served;
whether vengeance shines hot
or cold comets swerve.

And we never will climb
this mountain of skulls—
though we march to the heights
and we plod with these fools . . .
No, we never will climb
this mountain of skulls;
this pinnacle created
by the guns of the cruel.

We feel the crunch after
we set down our boots;
it echoes like laughter,
it chews through the roots.
Mexican children
melt death on their tongues—

and we never will reach them
as we slip from the rungs . . .

Because . . . you see . . .

We never will climb
this mountain of skulls—
though we march to the heights
and we plod with these fools . . .
No, we never will climb
this mountain of skulls;
this pinnacle created
by the guns of the cruel.

No, we never will climb
this mountain of skulls.

Lightless Oceans

Ann K. Schwader

The lightless oceans of our nightmares hold
a thousand shadows. Shaped by legends lost
to time or science, writhing in their cold
& utter void, they touch our minds with frost
past waking's warming. Yet this holocaust
of strange imagination fades away
before seas comprehended. Conquered. Crossed
off every list of myths—until one day
some minor moonlet cracks its crust, betrays
us into darkness. Far beneath that ice
flows living liquid, although life displays
no hint of the familiar here. Precise
as any apex nightmare, it awaits
our tardy understanding of man's fate.

The Dream-Wife

Adam Bolivar

The Devil was not done with Jack,
    And met him in the Square;
Mephisto's hat was high and black,
    His frock coat worse for wear.

"My name is Mister Scratch," he said.
    "My line is very old;
When other men are gone and dead,
    My tales will still be told."

"My tales will e'er be told as well,"
    Jack said then back to him.
"For I have plundered darkest Hell,
    And did so on a whim."

"Your tales indeed are quite well known,"
    The Devil so deferred.
Although the one where beans are sown
    I've always found absurd."

"Well, that was very long ago,"
    Jack said, and heaved a sigh.
"For though my tales will always grow,
    Myself, I soon shall die."

"I see you are a tad less spry,"
    Scratch snickered at poor Jack.
"I do not think I tell a lie
    To say you've lost your knack."

"'Tis true! 'Tis true! I'm old and gray;
    My wits are dull and cold;
It is December, not the May
    In which my tales are told."

"But after winter must come spring,"
    The Devil crowed with mirth.
"I find it such a cheering thing,
    Which proves that life has worth."

"But what is spring if I am dust?"
    Jack sadly shook his head.
"Bereft of life, of joy and lust,
    Beneath the ground and dead?"

"In dreams there is no need to die,"
    The Devil pressed his point.
"You have no need to moan and sigh;
    I shall not disappoint."

The horned one then produced a key,
    Of polished silver, old;
It conjured fancies just to see—
    About it tales are told.

It was the key to Jack's great house,
    Where lay in dreams a wife,
Who toyed with Jack, a cat her mouse,
    Her passion for him rife.

In dreams Jack was forever young,
    So trilled his balladress;
Eternal were the songs she sung,
    And scarlet was her dress.

Right there, Jack took the silver key—
    With Scratch, the deal was done;
Immortal now in dreams was he,
    And so, perhaps, he'd won.

More Than the Shark

M. F. Webb

Something is always in pursuit,
Though it frets and scatters at
Morning's clutch. Sleep is no disguise, no
Fished ember chars the clotted grotto where
It buries itself for you.

The clangor, the arrangement of
Filament and vein, the thread drawn red
Throughout, the pulse and raging. It pummels
Your ears, eats silence, with teeth
Of bronze and bells.

Rage is fuel for days, and food
That devours, accumulates in prologue.
The red dark loves you more than
It loves the shark. More than
The shark loves you.

The Embrace

Jessica Amanda Salmonson

Do not laugh at my withered arm.
Don't jest about my obsidian, lidless eyes.
Pretend not to see my hunchback,
My carbuncles, or my saggy dugs.
Tell me something kindly—
Tell me lies.

Don't flee in frightened alarm;
Fret not o'er the size of my teeth,
My slavered maw, my scaly jaw,
But see the sensitivity
Imprisoned and encumbered
Underneath.

Come unto me; find in me what charm
Resides within the gloomy hours of night,
Whimpers esoteric homilies, darkly recondite.
Gaze into these pools of liquid vision
That reflect you tiny
In my sight.

A Rude Awakening

Ian Futter

What wakes me in the night
isn't the alarm clock's jolting scream.
What fires and fuels my fright
isn't the dark shards of a dream,
or some splintered nightmare's scream.

What calls me from my sleep
is a movement from my bed.
It throws me from the deep
to the shallows of my head,
where I swim from sweat to dread.

And I wonder what it is
that could be crouching underneath,
knock, knock, knocking at my rest
and my sanity's relief
like the razors on a reef.

And I'm scared to look beneath,

where a beast upon his back
is surely kicking at the springs,
or some demons from hell's crack,
with their flapping beating wings,
are making room for other things.

All my screams are dead and dumb,
but I know that I must see,
so I bend to look below
and my dog runs out and flees
with more terror in his eyes

than the fear that falls from me.

For Sale

Deborah L. Davitt

At the shadow auction
there's no formula for free will,
just a marketplace for spirits,
otherworldly denizens
destined to be enslaved.

Efreet and djinn for sale
at the shadow auction,
crammed into bottles and lamps,
or, like cobbler elves,
forced to work naked for milk.

No labor laws for fey,
But all fairy tales are for sale
at the shadow auction.
Come see the russalka in her chains,
tears making her mascara run.

They only live for our convenience,
granting wishes and rewarding
virtue; find yourself a godmother
at the shadow auction,
and your future's set, assured.

Why work for success, or earn it,
when wishing's a certain cure?
Don't mind their tears or looks of dread.
Come on down and buy your fate
at the shadow auction.

Invocation to the Daemon for Modern Times

Liam Garriock

His shadow looms over the world
Like an eclipse, his eyes are sable moons
Or black mirrors. Amidst the impure tunes
On the radio, he whispers unfurled
Desires and secrets; his ghost is engraved
On the glass and the degraded concrete.
In his probing eyes, nothing is discreet,
No lust remains buried and no depraved
Act remains secret. All the empty cars,
Strewn across the dank marshes and desert,
Sit like women made barren by long wars;
The oozing bogs and spreading weeds, the dirt
Of a century destroyed by mad lust.
Metal starts to rust, bodies fade to dust.
He is the devil on the singer's back,
He is the leader of the human pack,
He is the demiurge who purges sin,
He is the worm under silicon skin,
He is the man whose legacy dies hard,
The king of dead futures—J. G. Ballard.

Aenid's Dream

Christina Sng

Aenid dreamed of stars
As I dream of death—
Peace is where it is.

I peel off layers from myself
And fold them gently
Into clouds.

They fall as rain, dissipating,
Till there is nothing left of me
But bone.

The breeze carries me
Past the exosphere
Far far away to the stars,

That Aenid dreamed of
A lifetime ago
In a different life.

The same dream of stars.

The God Within

Ronald Terry

Sleeping until the sun speaks,
hiding from my own shadow,
fire sprouts from my head
like a blooming rose
but burns nothing.

I'm not eternal
or anyone's savior,
just a shadow
that vanishes
in the light.

Wisdom is madness and grief
that torments you
to the edge of nothing.

I am my point of view
and nothing else.
Your hologram shimmers
in the sun like a rainbow.

I long to make it real,
as solid as my own thought,
born in blood
as surely as any infant
extracted from the void.

The Dark Pharaoh

Richard L. Tierney

Dark mage of ancient Stygia and Acheron,
    Thine awful thaumaturgies have for thee attained
Great powers, and for many ages thou hast reigned
    O'er empires fallen now into oblivion.

Thou didst invoke Nyarlat, that Mighty Messenger,
    Who set thee on Khem's throne in cruel and haughty pride
As Pharaoh Nephren-Ka, soon styled Death's Emperor!
    With his new Chosen One, Nyarlat is Satisfied.

Ave Augustissime: An Acrostic Sonnet on H. P. Lovecraft, Esq.

Manuel Pérez-Campos

How is it that thy handshake seems as if
press'd by one ris'n to haunt, and not long dead?
Lucid scribe of Angell St., thine each line's a riff
on ghoul'd drifts, thine each missive's Yrs for a dread
vista of starr'd gulfs that gyre without a plan.
Enrob'd entangler of tombs who, by wick-flame
crimp'd by unclos'd sills, evokes the rot of
rogue aeons with non-Euclidean élan:
Allow by dint of this thine encoded name—
fungi-dreamt—for us, cowl'd here at Innsmouth's cove,
to glimpse thee by some olde gate's mist again.
Enravish'd by thy warp'd imagin'd voice,
still we lust for more, that we may learn to ken
quaintly—and, in our own cursedness, rejoice.

Portrait of H. P. Lovecraft, Esq.: A Scrambled Acrostic Sonnet

Manuel Pérez-Campos

Omniloquent objector of the aeon!
Hysterical Hecate's dismal son!
Chronicler of somniloquies with shades!
Rhyparographer! Conjurer of Dagon!
Fear's amanuensis and mesmerist!
Encomiast of recluse renegades!
Arch-flamen of Azathoth pantokrator!
Lyre-wielding repeller of the night-gaunt's raids!
Eldritch teetotaler! Sanity's questor!
Star-deferr'd river self-annihilator!
Tartarus-dwelling epistolographist!
Ventorius vadelect of Poe's daemon!
Passéiste squire! Skald of sporif'rous tirades!
Quinible cat-summon'd noctambulist!

Dracul's Demesne

(A Sonnet Sequence)

Frank Coffman

I

In Transylvania's wild and widespread wood,
There stands a castle on a rocky steep.
Its crumbling walls a fearsome secret keep:
A horror not completely understood.

Although that looming fortress seems asleep,
The land around is soaked in human blood:
Thousands impaled, many the vampire brood
Claim—or kill—as they their harvest reap.

Long, long agone fierce, gory Dracul's days.
But some contend his soulless self remains,
Haunting the dark among those trackless ways.

Those few who live nearby, as daylight wanes,
Head homeward ere they see the sun's last rays,
Knowing that Night is when dread Evil reigns.

II

Where that great ruin with its tall spires looms
There flows below a gurgling rock-strewn stream.
The moonlight makes it sparkle like a dream,
But all around the Dark is full of dooms.

Into that castle grim the moon's wan beam
Shines through the widening gaps into dim rooms.
In one dark sanctum there, the floor entombs
His black heart that no magic can redeem.

He needs no heart who leads the pale undead,
Who slakes his horrid thirst with mankind's blood
And makes the living quake in terror and dread.

For centuries his kind have drawn a flood,
Not like the stream below, but gory red.
That Night belongs to Them is understood.

III

A few have tried that harsh, hard slope to dare
And climb up to that castle's gloomfast gate,
Knowing full well that they are tempting fate,
Knowing not whither thenceforth they may fare.

Some have been simply curious, but find too late
That there are things quite awful lurking there.
A few have passed one night but cannot share
The dreams they had—too dark to contemplate.

Some who have gone, their quest to put an end
To that foul master and his evil kind,
Found terrors with which no sanity could contend.

And those who dared thus died—or lost their mind.
An Evil that most cannot comprehend
Lurks in that place. And, dare you seek, you'll find.

IV

Below that castle crest the woods are dark.
Even at noon, so little light seeps through—
As if a giant, dark hand grasped and drew
A great veil across that woodland wide and stark.

But here and there, encircled, are a few
Small villages, cleared from the trees, that mark
The bold stand that the Living make. And hark!
Sounds of Life echo, colors of bright hue.

But well they know to shutter out the night
And homeward head when day's light turns to gloaming.
They know that darkness brings the ancient blight.

They've learned that twilight is the time for homing.
Long have they borne their ghastly, evil plight;
Never in darkness do they go aroaming.

V

That sylvan wilderness, when sun is gone,
Is home to forces preternatural.
Throughout its depths an ancient, evil pall
Falls all about and ceases not 'til dawn.

Then Dracul and his stregoii ilk and all
The Fiends of Darkness—everything that's thrawn—
Infest that realm and bring such horror on
That none can say what Evil might befall.

This is a land forlorn. The legends tell
Of the Dragon's Son and all his dreadful deeds—
And horrors dragged up from the depths of Hell.

Still he is here and often hunts and feeds.
Still often heard the knell of funeral bell.
And still the living mourn—and say their beads.

[The poem is composed in the Romanian sonnet form of Mihai Eminescu,
Romania's greatest verse poet. (The form: ABBA/BAAB/CDC/DCD with
separations into two quatrains and two tercets, all end-stopped and self-
contained in thought and statement.]

The Reaper's Garden

Ashley Dioses

In faded gardens blackened, stained with gray,
The purple belladonna and the rose,
Once blossomed beauties, started to decay.
Fair autumn's jacinth kiss turns chill, and grows
Still colder as the blight spreads bloom to bloom.
Then autumn paves the way for winter's cold,
The cruel caress that withers them in gloom,
Forever in the Reaper's deathly hold.

Testament of the Scribe

David Barker

I am passing through a land that is not my home, yet is hauntingly
familiar to me, for surely I sojourned here in another incarnation, and I
am eager to move on, so abhorrent is the thought of lingering. However,
some few persons whom I recognize as allies among the teeming throngs
of hostile strangers persuade me to tarry here a while longer, appealing
to my most lamentable spiritual weakness, an inordinate artistic pride,
placing in my hands thick sheaves of antique papers, illuminated codices
that once I scrawled in my wasted youth—rare narratives whose substance
I've forgotten, although the penmanship is undeniably mine.
Succumbing to vanity, I begin to sign these anonymous works, marveling
at the ornate lurid decorations I had emblazoned on each sheet. And
then I hesitate, wondering if I really ought to keep these lost relics of my
past, if I dare claim them at last and add them to my store of
accomplishments. But after scanning a particularly provocative passage, I
recall why I had abandoned these pernicious leaves in that other life I
now disavow—remember the reason I had left them scattered across a
wasteland whose air boasts the fragrance of a cloying tropical sweetness
and whose days are tempered by dissolute warmth: for these pages are
songs of an irredeemable decadence, verses of a feverish degeneracy, and
I shall not risk acknowledging them nor take pride in having fashioned
what is undeniably an instrument of my own damnation.

And I become aware of shadowy figures now gathering on the
periphery of the metropolis; the reckless arrogance of an impure heart
always draws them forth.

The pages slip from my hands, they flutter and fall from the parapet on whose allure I stand atop this rocky precipice, undulating like autumn leaves down the face of the walls and onto the waters below where their decaying husks will soon clot the drains. "Will you not sign?" my companions plead. "Will you not affix your name to these documents and own the truths they embody?" "No!" I proclaim as I pull away from their grasp. "I reject these abominable works! I denounce them as lies and vile seductions!" Sensing I will not be further detained, my erstwhile companions allow me to depart and instead turn to gathering what few pages I have not already tossed to the winds, believing them worthy of their veneration. I leave them to their foolish task, noticing as I place distance between us that certain stern beings well known to me have emerged as they will in such circumstances and are moving in stealthily from the dusky fringes of the hilltop enclave, murder burning brightly in their eyes, while others of this hooded tribe break away to follow me as they always have, insuring thus my continued wandering; for it is only through a resolute dedication to ceaseless movement and the rejection of all worldly vanities that I have been able thus far to escape the inevitable terrible reckoning these sanctified ones seek to deliver.

And now, above and behind me, from the crimson-stained streets of the high city come echoing anguished cries of mortal agony—the ultimate gasps of those unfortunates whose favor I had foolishly curried before I regained my composure and resumed my solitary pilgrimage.

The Graveyard Knows My Name

Ross Balcom

The graveyard knows my name.
It chants it night and day;
it scrawls it on headstones;
it breathes it into worms and bugs.

The graveyard knows my name.
It flashes it on my TV;
it bares it in my mirror;
it paints it in shadow on my face.

The graveyard knows my name.
It buries it letter by letter
in the kind and sheltering earth.
I will know rest. I will know stillness.

I am happy—happy
the graveyard knows my name.

Teratology

F. J. Bergmann

Sometimes in a spring night the air
is like a tincture administered invisibly,
in condensing dew; a posset of pennyroyal,
skunk cabbage and sassafras shoots infused
in thieves' vinegar, taken for its effects
under the white eye of the moon. You wade
through thickets, rustling down deer tracks
in the tingly dark. Something you have never
felt before squirms and somersaults
within your belly, fluttering and tickling
like the theligonum brushing your ankles.
What you needed went unspoken,
but she knew when you came to her door
in the dark and tentatively said you'd heard
she could . . . help. A tonic, she'd called
the drink. As if it were healthful. Inside you,
it is changing, growing long claws. Cramps
make you gasp and stagger; then the water
breaks, and it slithers out, gurgles, twitches,
stills. Blood flowing down your legs
like black tar in the moonlight. The blade-
edge of the shovel. The burying.

Repoman Homunculus

Chad Hensley

In an opulent penthouse of a particularly crooked Cyclopean tower,
Purple, serpent-shaped smoke coiled upwards toward the bejeweled
    ceiling,
Exhaled by a skeletally thin old man dressed in tattered black robes
Reclined on a couch of flayed human skins,
Relaxing from a hard week of necromantic exhumations in nether
    planes.

Outside on the window's gem-encrusted ledge, the darkness suddenly
    congealed
Into a miniature man with bat wings, body covered with reptilian scales
That sparkled in the sallow light of rotting corpses.
With a clenched fist, the tiny human shape tapped the dirty pane loudly,
His oversized smile a ratlike mouth of fangs
As his other hand pointed skywards.

Suddenly, a thousand desiccated troglodyte fists crashed through the
    ceiling.
The tower crumbled into a fine dust as it collapsed,
The old man laughed hysterically
As he somersaulted dodging the falling rubble:
He'd completely forgotten the thaumaturge's fee!

Imprisoned

Mary Krawczak Wilson

You cannot climb too high;
The fortress is made of steel,
Its windows are black and sealed,
And its walls are steeped in lye.

How do you emerge from hell?
Where is the exit to flee?
You scream out: "Let me be free!"
Echoes die in a dark cell.

The floor is icy and cold;
Hissing winds shatter your ears
And magnify every fear
Until your young soul grows old.

You yearn for rays of sunlight,
Yet only charred dust prevails;
It covers your face so pale—
Eyes blinded—you die from fright.

His Voice in the Whisper of Waves

Deborah L. Davitt and Kendall Evans

The ship with tattooed sails
enters the harbor at twilight;
the sails slowly lower,
while landing boats stay in place.
The inked sea monster
on one tattered canvas
and the faded dragon upon the other
flap in an uncertain breeze, and collapse.

High upon the castle watchtower
the princess keeps her view:
both hands uplifted,
one eye tight closed,
one eye pressed to a telescope.
Brought into sharpest focus,
the ship's crew seems as tattered as the sails;
the hand of one crewman,
raised high to grip a braided rope,
is a skeleton's, void of flesh.

Her prince is aboard the vessel—
provided he did not perish
somewhere far out to sea.
Have his eyes become pearls?

Are his bones picked clean
and neatly arranged
in some mermaid's sandy
meandering garden
deep on the floor of the sea?

She hopes her prince is well
and not so motley as his crew.
With eager dread she meets them on the quay
and listens as fingerbones rattle
words on teeth and ribs,
thus describing their journey—

A storm took us, and we foundered;
we gave our cargo to the waves
to save our lives,
gave our coin to the locals
to repair the hull,
gave our skin to the bo'sun
to replace our sails,
gave our flesh to the gods
to make the wind blow.

The prince waits in his cabin;
the lantern sways, the shadows shift.
Her prince, she sees, is not so sorry

as is his osseous crew;
his face and hands are fleshed,
although an ivory bone protrudes
from one necrotic fingertip.

Trembling, she tries to meet his gaze—
those milky eyes are mirrors to no soul.
His lips are cyanotic blue,
his dead heart does not beat,
and his voice is the whisper of waves.

My beautiful one,
can you still love a man
reduced to these essentials,
be it life in death or death in life?
If so, please take what's left of me
and make of me your own.

Mary of the Rosy Grave

K. A. Opperman

Mary 'neath the weeping willow,
Mary of the rosy grave,
I would make for me a pillow
'Mid your bosom's ivory nave.

Mary in your ruby bedding,
Mary like a moon-white gem,
Soon shall be our blessèd wedding,
Mushroom-ring our diadem.

Mary, dead and yet undying,
Mary, uncorrupt of rot,
I have heard you softly sighing
In your warm and perfumed plot.

Mary, I have heard the demon;
Mary, does he tell me lies?
Mary, make of me your leman—
Mary, drink my soul and rise.

—After "The Lay of Dumah" by Adam Bolivar

Things Come out of the Fog

G. O. Clark

Things come out of the fog,
grotesque, unnatural atrocities,
voiceless, faceless nightmare things
clawing their way into the real.

Things that don't go bump
in the night, seek out the jugulars
of the innocent, or hide in the shadows
of schools and shopping malls.

Things just wanting back into
this realm, to escape from their cells
of eternal darkness, to fit in with the
new normal, senses on fire.

Preference for human flesh
a longstanding culinary tradition,
the current menu of this world a
cornucopia of possibility.

Moment

Nathaniel Reed

Fragments remain where filaments
Once held the finite and fragile earth.
Bound by nothing, the planet rolls
Without pause into the expanse.

Silence envelops. Its grasp smothers
The lone and final ruins of animation.
As the sun becomes a distant dream,
A shattered world fades into extinction.

Ad'Naigon

Maxwell I. Gold

I remembered, fearfully so, on that day when past the hungering blackness, its spectral breath wheezed with a sighing blast that made all the stars adhere to the shining yellow radiance that was so brilliant and so terrifying.

On the streets the old skyscrapers stood; on the streets the towers waned toward the blasphemous skies that began to echo with cries that reflected off the golden dust. I walked alone . . . alone into the chaotic streets; crowded with a populace that, too, was fearful of the yellow sky. From the deepest parts of cosmic space, past all the lost cries of monstrous cosmogonies, the yellow disfigurement had been awakened. Ad'Naigon, atop his throne of marble and ivory, in a place unscalable in thought, stirred—and the voids shuttered.

It was with a heavy heart that I saw the world divulge into such a frenzy. This was not the first time the yellow wrath of that ancient horror had plagued our earthly realm. From the earliest known records of our most primitive human ancestors, brief flashes of its memory lingered in dreams and thoughts; whether it may have been the delusionary outcries from those outcasts of our primordial founders or some warning; it was ignored. The skies bled with that same yellow dust that floated into the eyes of all who were hypnotized by its odd phosphorescent glow. And so too, in dream, did my mind become filled with visions of what was to come. No one would dare listen to my warnings or cries.

From the howling aeons, deserts turned to glass and trees were uprooted in furious rage; all seemed overwhelmed as the vaulted firmament cracked under the sorrowful weight of golden stardust.

Nature was defiled, construed into a hellish fury, as I felt the radiant shutter of that yellow glow. I remembered, on that day when the stars rained their contemptuous fury, unabashed by the light of the pasty dust that floated hauntingly in the last moments of my thoughts, when the last fragments of my mind were finally strewn across space and time; when I too would become dust, drifting in the ghostly embers of cosmic voids whereupon I would reach the halls of that blighted thing at the ancient ends of Time.

In the cities of my home, the chaos of the immensity was so great, it appeared that the terror was beyond comprehension—no order or conceivable sense of balance. There was nothing left, no thought or consciousness, where any discernible person could attempt to see in the world he once knew, before the flicker of that horrid glow. There was nothing left of me. . . .

Doll in the Wall

Jessica Amanda Salmonson

Polly, me dolly,
I sealed her in the wall;
And when I took her out again
'Twas not the same at all.
She didn't seem to like me,
She tried to do me harm;
And so I set her hair aflame,
Which set off an alarm.

So now I think me Polly
Is pondering me doom;
I see her by the dim night-light
Walking in me room.
Slash! she goes and Gash! she goes
And hacks me into bits,
Then seals me pieces in the wall
Until I've lost me wits.

From the Yellow Text of Thanos Khan

Don Webb

R'lyeh doesn't lie in an earthly sea;
it lies in the blood of you and me,
writing to burst as a nightmare rose.

R'lyeh doesn't lie in an earthly sea;
Its strange angles spiral chaotically,
Built by forces slower than time.

It lies within you and me;
dreams lie that blame the sea
and hide the fact of our darkness.

R'lyeh doesn't lie in an earthly sea;
it waits for your yearning mind to set it free;
it waits for the artist to say the words,

"It lies within you and me."
This spell is the silver key
that unlocks the once and future door.

You've read the words and started the process;
the Old Ones' priest will have his success.
R'lyeh doesn't lie in an earthly sea;
it lies within you and me.

Angry Sun/Bloated Moon

Claire Smith

A bloated moon hangs in the sky.
My tears flood. I keep a record—
Red pastel splashes on a black wall—
The days, months . . . The years we've been apart.

I bask
A warm Icarus
Before his wings caught fire; melted—
He flew too near to the Sun when it got angry.

Freedom?
You had it.
All of it: Larks to sing you to sleep,
Dove-down pillows to comfort your head,
And Swan guards to keep you safe.

You took me to the coast:
Among Eagles. They circled near
Above the cliffs, Gulls who stole
And the Night Shade—
You gave me my first taste of Death.

I hear the tales of your innocence all the time,
Along the broken lines of gossip,

You know, how I ruined you . . .
A bee left its sting
In your honey-dew covered skin.

Was I the bluebottle hung—
Trapped In your snare?
A fly stuck fast in chains . . .
A fly's body embedded in silk ties . . .
A fly torn to pieces in the jaws of a spider . . .

You burnt yourself. You let *my* drink
Slide from your mouth,
Down your oesophagus,
To the pit of your stomach . . .
You screamed . . . It fastened to your organs
(Never wretch and cough)
You retched *and* you coughed!

Secret Tree

John Shirley

In a forest nigh to Yorkshire
strange customs yet endure
—some meant to quell uneasy graves.
But the story I'm called to tell
is of a tree that can't be felled;
of blood that branches even as it craves.
There the Ancient of the Woods
is masked by a tattered hood
so that passersby will not see his gnarl;
and most who come his way
he simply drives away
with a damning curse and a cursing snarl.
But one day came a youth
seeking his ancestral truth—
it was hidden much like the old man's face.
His mother felt a shame—
would not speak his father's name—
but said, "The Twisted Tree is your birthplace."
So journeyed the youth thither
—the young man's name was Mither—
asking where the Twisted Tree was found.
With shaking heads and shaking fingers
(not wanting him to linger)
they bade him, "Follow ye yon weeping sound."
And through the forest he proceeded

till the weeping that he heeded
took him to a twisted willow tree:
a knotted tree which wept
when breezes sighed and swept
through sunless glades to the black stone scree.
He beheld the storied Ancient,
always seated, always patient—
Mither felt a strange and instant bond;
the youth hailed him as he knelt,
and said, "I am a wandering Celt
who seeks in what manner he was spawned."
The Ancient spoke in growls
and in the shriek of angry owls,
and then drew back his tattered hood.
Mither gasped to see
the Ancient gnarled as the willow tree
Twisted like the tangles of his fate;
the Ancient said, "Every man who lives
has somewhere a tree that gives
the shape of his every ugly trait.
And each tormented role
shows in the knotted bole
of a man's secret twisted tree.
I have found my own;
I take its gnarls into my bone

as I wait here on the black stone scree.
I've been waiting for my son,
for he's the only one
who can take my place between these tortured roots.
And when he replaces me
he'll twist like his secret tree—
which grew in pain from his writing shoots."
The youth then turned to run,
ran till the setting of the sun—
when he fell beneath a youthful spruce;
he recognized the tree,
knew it was his destiny—
his secret tree would never let him loose.

Only 13

Ian Futter

What monster snatched him
away from the light?
What black, bloody claws
dragged him far from my sight?

What rank, rotted hull,
fixed with funeral bell,
wrenched my hand from his hand
as it sailed off to hell?

What soft sliming spit
sealed his face up with glue,
took his voice from my ears,
and his ears from mine, too?

What terrors from time
took my friend, in that hour,
from the sun of my eye
to some fog-shrouded tower?

Now I'm lonely and lost,
with a scream in my head.

"You shouldn't feel like that
about a boy."

My dad said.

Expanding Universe

Ronald Terry

The disintegration of power
yields undying strength
to transcend thought.

My mother used to sing to me;
Now she sings only to herself,
long ago descended
into her own mind,
spellbound by fragments
of vast repeating mirror images
rising from fallen gravestones,
all the years of birth and death
faded by stubborn wind and rain.

Fire flares up from within,
consumes all but the outer skin,
which waves in the wind
until its ashes scatter to nothing
or a new universe,
its particle constellations
light-years apart and
unknown to one another.

As if glimpsed within a storm,
the Fates stop dancing

for one moment,
swirling skirts falling stiff,
weeping over a minor chord,
crushed by the rising
fog of silence.

The Final Turn

Ann K. Schwader

The story at its start is innocent
enough: a governess, a pair of children
sequestered in the countryside where secrets
root deepest. Throw in rumors of a death
or two, an honest housekeeper still haunted
by something subtle. Shadows of the damned

begin their flickering at windows, damned
anew by hope. Such flawless innocent
young vessels fairly cry out to be haunted,
yet none suspect how quickly. Why should children
so sheltered, so protected offer death
a set of playthings? Surely nursery secrets

suffice. Too soon for twilight with its secret
anticipations . . . assignations . . . damned
& damning consequences. Let the death
of candor come to other innocents,
but spare these two: so guardians, like children
themselves, weave fantasies against the haunted

inevitable dark. Where lives are haunted
by silence, these conspiracies of secrets
may pass unnoticed. Only ghosts & children

slip through illusion, choosing to be damned
instead by truth, the brutal innocence
of what cannot be changed. Presuming death

is silent also, that no tongue of death
might find a living speaker leaves the haunted
adrift within themselves, too innocent
to know their own corruption. Keeping secrets
becomes a creeping habit, no less damned
for being charming—charming as these children

worn now as masks by phantoms playing children
against approaching autumn, flaunting death
from every windowpane & tower. Damned
as disbelievers, fragile allies haunted
in every sense must resurrect the secret,
deny the obvious. The innocent.

And with the dawn, these shells of children haunted
by selfish death surrender every secret,
leaving survivors damned by innocence.

—After Henry James's *The Turn of the Screw*

Arrival

M. F. Webb

It will not be enough to say your name
Or call you as a guest. You will intrude
to make each corner perilous, and claim
my sleeping and my bathing and my food.

I must recollect the leaves that grow through
earth and stone in parallel unfolding.
Every cell and countenance must know you
before I see futility in holding

what has moved beyond the earthly graces,
what is written in the planet's turning:
Mystery that hides from human faces,
secrecy embodied in my yearning.

My guest, you saturate my every skin.
My enemy: today I let you in.

He Dreams of Beauty

Liam Garriock

The artist dreams of beauty. All his young life he has dreamt of emerald fields underneath starry violet skies, where cool breezes winnow through the grass and a mighty tower of jade glints in the distance. He paints on his canvas far lands of the East, kissed by a blazing sun, that are told of only in elder legends and tales, where caravan-drivers seek kingdoms and cities crowned by golden pinnacles, and honey-skinned goddesses with hair of fire and ice dance in the rippling sunlight. He craves the wells whence the maidens have drunk. He seeks to swim in the cool azure oceans where the garnet-studded temples of Neptune stand underneath. And most of all, he pines for the unattainable Goddess of All, wispy as a fey dream, with navel and nipples of jacinth, and eyes of zircon, a fading sky of summer.

Alas! the artist dreams of corruption. His mind is drawn to the ravenous worms that dwell in violated flowers, to the golden and ghostly succubae that drift from unfrequented gardens of rotting foliage. The lithe vampire-slugs dance in front of his eyes like reflections in the deep blue water, and a callous moon looms over him in the black and starless skies. Everywhere he goes, he sees the gnawing invisible insects that crawl and slither over everything, and he cannot banish them from his sight. And through all this charnel melancholy, wandering through a city founded on sodomy and debauchery like a lost soul, the artist can see the great and presiding goddess who haunts him. She is a gigantic, glistening Worm masquerading as a beautiful woman who swims in a sea of urine; her wine is the tears of poets and her food is the hearts of men and women and the excrement of soulless cities. Even as he strives to reach the rainbow-coloured world his heart pines for, he can never escape the grasp of the underlying, presiding darkness that is everywhere and nowhere.

Pull

Christina Sng

Each night
I pull the leeches
From my throat;

They squeal
And bleat
As they exit.

That night
I will sleep
A dreamless sleep

Of bliss
As only
I know.

One night
I forget
And fall asleep.

I dream
Of eating
My bones.

Since then
I've never forgotten
That terrible dream

And at bedtime,
I pull
And pull.

Innsmouth Shanty

David Barker

Briny devils from the sea
Think they own a piece of me.
At their bidding I will come,
Flipping through the tide like chum,
Sinking in the ocean's chalice,
Slipping down to Dagon's palace.

[Refrain:] So rally, boys, at Innsmouth
To frolic 'neath the waves;
And drink brown ale,
Then we'll set sail—[1]
We'll not be any man's slaves!

The sea, like wine, inebriates,
The salt-rich air intoxicates.
Hybrid fools of dire estate
Beneath the waves must congregate.
Moved by forces in the blood,
To wallow in the sea floor mud.

[Refrain:] So rally, boys, at Innsmouth [etc.]

---

[1] Note: A bawdy variant has the line "Chase fishy tail—" instead of "Then we'll set sail—"

Frog-fish maids from South Sea isles
Lure us with their wanton wiles.
How can mortal men resist
Once they have been mermaid-kissed?
Into the deep we swim to spawn
In this, our final liaison.

[Refrain:] So rally, boys, at Innsmouth [etc.]

Begetting offspring by the score,
Into our nets finned schools do pour.
Our wives and daughters are bedecked
In gold from galleys that were wrecked
Upon the shoals past Devil Reef
Where many a sailor came to grief.

[Refrain:] So rally, boys, at Innsmouth
To frolic 'neath the waves;
And drink brown ale,
Then we'll set sail—
We'll not be any man's slaves!

Metamorphosis

Frank Coffman

The first time that he changed was horrible,
Worse than the rest—because it was the first.
Without, the night was clear, the moon was full.
It had begun as an agonizing thirst—
But not for water. A lust for human blood
Rose up in him, until a ruddy cloud
Behazed his vision; then a rising flood
Of rage and pain; and then—most long and loud—
He howled. The transformation started quick,
As limbs and head began their awful change:
His face grew forth, his sinews knotted thick,
His form and frame began to rearrange,
Coarse hair pushed through where once the naked skin
Of what was human but a while before,
Where late the artful fingers of a man had been
Curved claws protruded now—and what was more—
His blue eyes turned to red and glinted bright,
His voice a growl most inarticulate.

Then, somewhat like a man, he rose upright
And went out through the door into the night,
Running across the yard, out through the gate.
No longer manlike in his loping shape.
Still dim in him a thought cried out, "Escape."
But it was far too late to turn back then—

Either to home or to his human skin.
That night his need for blood and death began
His curse to deal foul death—yet not in Sin.

That bite he'd suffered but four weeks ago,
Ere he had killed that wolf with one strong blow,
Had festered first, yet healed so soon and strange.
He'd clubbed the creature with his silver cane—
But, strangely, the spot where it had lain
Was barren when he led them back again
To where he'd killed it. And the wound did change
Most oddly: burning at first, hot fever coming on;
Within a week a scar was formed—then gone!
Leaving the faintest outline on his flesh
That seemed to grow more definite and fresh—
How strange! A nearly perfect pentacle—
As the new moon slowly widened to the full.

Awakened the morning after that first time
By singing birds, the wetness of the dew,
His clothing torn and bloody, soaked with gore,
Out in the forest past the parkland wide
That fronted his estate, his hideous crime
Was dim and hazy. For the human knew
Nothing of, as a beast the night before,

The horror he had wrought. The man had cried
In terror to see "A wolf?" "A man!" "A thing?"

He'd waited for what the next full moon might bring.
Again and always the changing was the same.
No way to still the moon's slow steady path;
Always the time would pass, the full moon came
To leave its awful, grisly aftermath.

And, over time—but not so *very* soon—
He grew resigned—then longed for that big moon.

The Wyrde of the Bibliognost; or, Another Solitude

Manuel Pérez-Campos

Curs'd the she-freak who loves olde books
and tow'rs them by her piss-stain'd bed—
nor cares not that her unkempt looks
            make her seem dead;

who breathes in with tranc'd delight
those half-page moulds which rhapsodize
of towns that are by taper'd light
            a feast to flies;

for whom each is a gilt-stitch'd corpse;
who—though her fake long lashes sag—
claws forth with each in intercourse
            like some shunn'd hag;

who from her thick-cak'd per'wig picks
bulg'd ticks to munch or make converse
with—fiends of shrewd can't-catch-me tricks
            whose blood is hers.

She is the sovran of her vault—
but ay, when the tow'rs all, by George,
drop on her till her twitchings halt—
            the rats will gorge!

Silent Songs

Deborah L. Davitt

Floating in the silent buoyancy
of liquid methane and ether,
below the surface of a glass-clear sea,
suit heaters strain to keep me warm and alive.

Twenty meters up, my partner and I
had leaped from the ship into the waves,
catching a last glimpse of the golden streak of dawn
against the haze-bronze horizon
before the hydrocarbon clouds swept in,
returning day to this moon's eternal night.

Giant shapes rose from depths unfathomed,
outlined in the glow of bioluminescent bacteria,
leviathans, shimmering like crystal, silicone beauty;
their long tentacles fractal in their frost-rimed symmetry,
perhaps a kilometer long, each—

Their wide mouths bloomed like flowers;
when they pushed the water through,
their entire bodies became sounding boards,
fretting the frozen sea with interlacing chords;
tentacles coiled, flashing with internal lights and colors.

Even through my suit, my bones sang their song,
my teeth rattled in rhythm;
my heart stuttered, threatened to stop;
my whole body thrummed
as I dissolved into the sensation,
feeling what the thunder spoke.

The Ballad of the de la Poers

Adam Bolivar

The de la Poers in Exham did
    In baron's state once dwell:
A priory whose walls had hid
    A curse from darkest Hell.

The only living de la Poer
    From England swiftly flew,
For all his kith and kin the lore
    Averred he foully slew.

Americans his heirs became,
    Still secretive by trait;
These Delapores were much the same,
    Bequeathed a loathly fate.

Three hundred years had nearly passed,
    When I, the heir, returned,
And Exham was restored at last,
    Which still the peasants spurned.

The memory of folk is long,
    And I was much disdained,
My ancestors reviled in song,
    My reputation stained.

The priory was built upon
    An ancient temple's stone,
Where blood was spilt before the dawn—
    A secret now unknown.

Now in my new-built hall I dwelt,
    A proper de la Poer,
As had the Saxon and the Celt,
    And those who came before.

At night my cat was sorely vexed
    By rats within the wall,
Whose passage left me much perplexed,
    And led beneath the hall.

When daylight came I searched the vault
    With Norrys by my side,
A steadfast friend with little fault,
    Who with me would abide.

A Roman temple lay within
    Where Atys was adored,
Where rites were held of blackest sin,
    And decency deplored.

We slept in there, my friend and I,
    To dream of fungous swine;
The rats returned: we heard them fly,
    And scratch beneath the shrine.

To London then we hied in haste
    To find some learned men,
Who would not shrink when they were faced
    With evil in its den.

So seven men then probed the pit
    Through Magna Mater's maw,
And afterwards none would admit
    The truth of what they saw.

We crept down stone and time-worn stairs
    Beneath the Roman tile,
To meet with ape-like skulls' dull stares,
    Their cretinism vile.

The twilit grotto from my dream
    Was there, my God it was!
We saw in torches' spectral gleam
    Bones pocked by rodents' gnaws.

A Saxon house, the swineherd's lair,
    Who kept the fungous beasts
In ruins where the noxious air
    Still smelt of daemon feasts.

The rats returned to lead me on
    To ecstasies of old,
Into the brink, the inky yawn,
    Where hunger took ahold.

'I'll learn ye how to gust at me,
    At what my kinsmen do . . .
For ev'ry man must eaten be—
    Thou stinkards know 'tis true!

"For Magna Mater, Atys's sake
    Agus bas dunach ort!
My herd of swine a feast shall make,
    And eat you for their sport."

They found me then crouched o'er the corpse
    Of Norrys, once my friend;
My fiendish face still madness warps,
    My freedom at an end.

And all the rats, I hear them still!
    They scamper in the walls. . .
Into my bones they bring a chill;
    In dreams the swineherd calls.

Corridors Enough

Ann K. Schwader

The brain has corridors enough
To host a hundred ghosts of selves
Outgrown, outlasted, or rebuffed.
The brain has corridors enough,
But doors & windows? Missing. Tough
To exorcise such bitter elves:
The brain has corridors enough
To host a hundred ghosts of selves.

—After Dickinson

The Daughter of Death

Charles D. O'Connor III

Don't let me sleep; I dread yet another encounter with the daughter of death. Every night she lures me onto her satin bed woven in many-colored dreams; hues and dimensions that are seen by mortals—lovely spiritual dust sparkling, blessing, calling and enchanting; celebrating the moments a person flickers on the air before father death blows you out like candles on a birthday cake.

But when I lie down on her satin bed blackness blinds my eyes and its rusty coffin slams shut—I'm unable to wake up. How many souls suffer inside their caskets from similar abuse; banging, scratching, leaving marks in crimson gore? Nobody knows, because we never hear them shriek. They are silent, or perhaps fast asleep.

And nobody hears me when I shriek—helpless and frightened before the daughter of death. She hovers above, wrapping the slimy carapace of the woman I loved around her rotting, inky form; the woman who tormented my soul and dragged it down to die among dim valleys of despair. The likeness is incredible. It paralyzes my body, eating its way through my brain like an earwig, leaving anguished memories behind like filth strewn across flowers.

Now my lips tremble, begging and pleading to God. Yet the rotting thing descends, wrapping its beautiful guise around my head, squeezing like an anaconda. Then it seeps inside, sucking and engulfing all energy, all life; weighing on my soul like an immense burden.

I have escaped from beneath this burden many times and woken up in the living, breathing, mortal world that shines golden with promises of tomorrows yet to come. But I never breathe peacefully, because the memory of the woman I loved still haunts me. She is a solid personification of the *Keres*—female death spirits in Greek mythology. Still, I do anything to forget; believing my lack of attention to her might strangle her memory, relegating it to a dim, forgetful past. Instead, my enslaved brain returns to Nyx, the personification of night where sleep, *Hypnos*—the daughter of death—waits to assume the semblance of that awful woman I once loved so I'll weaken and she can drink all my energy and life.

I struggle to avoid sleep but always succumb to her allurement in the end. And when I awaken, I feel drained; sometimes I can't remember where I live or even my own name. Now my identity is growing hazy. All I remember is the woman I loved and the daughter of death, or *Hypnos*—the name she has taken on. I'm not safe. It won't be long before I forget everything and only remember her . . . the daughter of death.

Under the Blood Moon

Sunni K Brock

I painted flowers for you
Cleansed my blade in sage

I spoke to the spirits
East West North South appeased

I let my blood into the cup
Blessed it in your name

I topped the cup with fine red wine
Muttering my final wish

Will you do the honor
And make a toast for posterity?

Her Skull and the Sea

Mary Krawczak Wilson

She was always known to roam
Far from her baptismal home,
Beyond the meadows and moors
To reach the sea's briny shores.

She inhaled the salty air,
Exposing her skin so bare
Against the bleached, grainy sand;
A hollow skull lay inland.

She peered into opaque eyes
Barren and black lit, but wise;
Could her cracked cranium quote
Profound words that she once wrote?

She yearned to cradle the dead
And infuse the words she once said,
Thereby becoming as one,
Her twin now scorched by the sun.

What It Means When You Dream of Swords

F. J. Bergmann

You are walking through an armory. The light
is almost not light. There are swords in scabbards,
swords hung on walls or clasped in armored hands,
rusting blades scattered on the stone floor. You are
searching for something vital that you cannot find.

You have stolen a sword, a beautiful silver blade,
sharp as pain, straight as the horizon of a still sea,
its hilt studded with sapphires and bound with the hide
of a manticore. You hide it beneath your fur surcoat,
against your warm skin, and it begins eating you alive.

A small hand clings to your left hand; you grip a sword
in your right. The blade is black with blood. Flames rise
all around you, and you are running, running as fast
as you can through the smoke and the screaming.
Then the small hand slips out of your hand.

The water is wide, you are pursued and desperate,
and you are grateful to see the boat drawn up on shore
with the boatman waiting for you. But the boat is full
of swords whose weight would sink it—and someone
has thrust a heavy claymore down through its hull.

You come home somehow, late, exhausted, and cold.
All the lamps are lit, but the house is empty. You go
from room to room, your weary footsteps echoing,
until you come at last to your desolate bedchamber.
On one side of the coverlet lies a naked sword.

The weapon you seek has more than two edges.
You might have known what would come of getting
your heart's desire. You cannot hold what doesn't
want to be held. It is not yet time to cross the river.
You lie down next to the sword and close your eyes.

My Beloved Bones

Jessica Amanda Salmonson

*"It ain't no sin to take off your skin
and dance around in your bones."*

While I was asleep, my skeleton
Climbed out through my mouth
To go dancing in the starlight
Laughing at the far, far light.

The New Moon was a hole in the sky,
A black, black hole
Where the stars are bright.

The skeletons of sleeping cats
Joined the dance
With arched spines
And teeth shining
Like adders' fangs,
Wind whistling through
The sockets of their eyes.

The rats are wide awake
To take what they can take,
Riding in my vagrant skeleton's ribs,
Skittering in joy,
Clinging tight or bouncing high
And chittering, "Ahoy!"

The lucent stars are fire-drops
On the sea. My skeleton skips
Along the margins of the tide
With clacking cats in tow, with
Rats upon their backs
Tittering, "Ahoy! Ahoy!"

A one-eyed owl that never hoots,
It clicks and screeches, snicks and toots
With broken wing, it cannot fly,
So running swiftly near the tide
Behind the bone parade, forsooth
A ratty meal reflecting in its eye.

Back up my skeleton's legs
The rats clamber and soon reside anew
In jolly ribs, to foil the owl that hops
Upon a cat of bones,
Talons against kitty-claws,
Bones and feathers scattered.
Somewhere alley cats
Like furry jellyfish,
They will wake at dawn
And yowl in terror,
Their bones forever gone.

All the while I lay abed
In a dream of whimsy and the dead,
My face without a skull
Grinning hugely, toothless, dull—
Lo! A cacophony of birds
Singing in the garden,
Prelude to sunrise, O! Beloved Bones!
Return to me! Come home! Come home!
Into my gaping maw, feet first,
And pull me on like tight pyjamas.

Ow! Ow-ow! A rat is feasting on my heart!
Oh, foolish bones, you've killed us,
Or if only me, then you will
Lie below the sod, encoffined
Far from Dis or God, no prancing
In the New Moon's starlight with your
Kittens anymore.

Rising Damp

M. F. Webb

The stain has reached the window sill,
The mold has crawled into the beams;
I've had them out to dig until
They've taken out the very seams

Of soil that first I did suspect.
And still, without that loathsome mud
I do not get what I expect
Or see the evidence of flood

That nightly rumbles in the walls,
That daily churns beneath the floor.
I tell myself 'tis damp, that's all,
'Tis natural and nothing more.

And yet somehow I still discern
That something lurks that means me ill.
Perhaps 'tis best I do not learn
What flows beneath the window sill.

Night Terrors

Ian Futter

I froze last night
again.
I don't like to recall it:
A sleeper bound
within his bed;
locked panic paused;
so close to dead,
not breathing.

But something breathing
near, so near,
within, without;
a hissing fear was rising—

and though I struggled
hard to turn,
my head was lead
and like my body
mocked me
for its lack of life
or movement.

And so I squirmed
within this case;
bone-basket stilled
with functional face,
not breathing.

Nor daring for a breath
to clear,
in case that breath should
catch the ear
of that strange shape
that was without
and by my bedside,
crouching.

David Lynch

Liam Garriock

You are driving through a desert at night. The starry darkness is then
pierced by the bright lights of a lone diner. You enter this diner and see
the sparse customers, who look as though they all have tales to tell. One
man, in particular, catches your interest: he has grey hair and is wearing
a black suit, and he casually smokes a cigarette, and a cold cup of coffee
and a half-eaten meal rest in front of him. You sit down and order a coffee,
which you do not touch, for there is some strange and undefined dread
tugging at you; you cannot quite remember what it is, but you sense that
you might be trying to escape it. By the time you remember what it is,
the man in the black suit is sitting directly in front of you, elbows on the
table, his face eagerly peering into yours. He wants to hear your story,
and he wants to hear it now; and before you have a chance to protest, a
great hand (from him?) reaches for your face and covers your eyes.

Sitting alone in the dark and unkempt room, static droning on the
television, you know why you are there. Outside the lone window, it is
dark, no stars, no lights from any neighbouring buildings or familiar
midnight establishments. Moths flutter around the dim light hanging
like a radiant corpse from the dirty, dingy ceiling, like lost planets
orbiting a perishing sun. You are sitting on the settee; a few holes where
the stuffing shows through are visible. That figure in the black suit
sitting in the dark corner, can you be sure if he is here for you? How can
you be sure if what you see is real or not? The static on the television,
awaiting a broadcast that shows the end of the world. The telephone on
the table, awaiting a burbling voice on the other side to announce that
everything is finished before the line drops dead. Maybe you will wait
forever; and as you wait for the end, or for someone to collect you, or

anything, you see phantoms gliding past you, emissaries from unknown chambers in turbid red gloom. If you see their faces, you might recognise them, or you might not. Perhaps you should just fall asleep and dream, dream of wide stages where illogical plays are performed. The audience come in many shapes and sizes and colours, but they all share the same stony glare as each act ends and the curtain falls; they all mechanically applaud because someone or something expects them to. Like the actors, the audience are bit-players in some random, comical, poignant, meaningless drama whose scope encompasses the whole universe. Your life is part of this epic absurdist drama, and everyone you have ever known has his or her parts to play, too. You know the dreadful truth about your life and everyone else's, and you have always known it; but every time you find out, you are powerless to do anything about it. You have seen the one responsible for weaving this web of horror and deceit around you; you have seen him at parties, behind the wall of the restaurant, in the idyllic small towns surrounded by forests of Douglas firs, in the house next door to you, on the cold plains of the moon through your telescope. Behind his smiles lurk diabolic plans to abuse you, make a mockery of your existence. Who would have thought that that dead leaf on the ground or that insect on the wall was conspiring against you? When you die, instead of letting your soul expire into a blissful nothingness, he puts your soul in another body and causes you to relive the whole trauma and melancholy over and over again until the great end of everything when even they fall into the abyss. You might travel to some far and remote location to confront the one who is doing all this, but he always expects you, and he pacifies you with all the things your heart pines for. You are powerless—everyone is powerless. Some people can only imagine and guess. The world is a nebulous fever-dream in the rotting skull of David Lynch.

It's Hell Being Your Guardian Angel

John Shirley

I'm more a drinker than a drugger
(Ma said don't do either one)
I'm a whiskey slugger—
and I'm a hellion with a gun.

But when I found the den for opium
In the basement of a bar,
I thought, "I have traveled plenty
but I haven't gone that far."

And always go a little farther:
That is the spin upon my ball;
So I bought a pipe-full, then two more—
and watched movies in the walls.

Devils danced, and rode a dragon
—I chased the dragon, time or two;
And an ape declaimed a sermon—
then an angel flew into view.

His voice came to me loud and clear—
he leaned all weary on a star;
"I am your guardian angel—
and this has gone too far.

"God may be a phantasm
  For I am no way Heaven-sent;
  But your mother asked me to guide you
  as I was dying, before I went.

"It's Hell to be your angel,
  It makes me sick to watch:
  Oh, how you overdo it
  when you're pouring down the Scotch.

"And now it's juice of poppy
  for an addict in the making—
  Only so much a ghost can bear;
  My heart's near to breaking."

I said, "Hey, my guardian angel,
  set down there in that chair."
He floated to it with a sigh—
  said, "I guess that's only fair."

He nestled nigh, like smoke himself,
Said, "It's enough you puff that tar.
I hate it too when you decide
  to have a run out in your car."

I asked, "What the Devil is so wrong
with a man driving his own car?"
Said he, "But yesterday you drove it
through the windows of a bar!"

Criticism's hard to bear
From angelic ectoplasm—
So I grabbed him up and pressed him down
without a guilty spasm.

I tucked him down into my pipe
And lit his spirit alight;
He was a darn good smoke, was he—
quite took me to the heights.

The Spiders of Kepler 452B

Kendall Evans

The spiders of Kepler
452b
Are not intelligent—
It is the webs they weave
Intricate, expansive,

Sheathed in silk,
Neurological impulses flow
Through silver filaments—
The webs are sentient,
Conscious, and dreaming,
Scheming, configuring.

The alien arachnids
On 452b
Are symbiotic avatars
& the interwoven webs
Perceive their world
Via spiders' eyes.

Classic Reprints

Amenophra*

Ernest A. Edkins

There are rare moments in this earthly life,—
In this terrestrial arc of being—rife
(E'en as they fade away, we shrink aghast!)
With shrouded phantoms of an unknown past.†
Unknown, I say,—yet to the eye they seem
Strangely familiar, while that fleeing dream
Holds us beneath its spell; in such brief space
As marks the second-hand's erratic race
Once 'round the smaller dial, or twice, perchance,—
We sink, in breathless horror, 'neath the trace,
We faint, and yet the helpless body falls
(It seems for hours!) between green chasmal walls
Of polished, gleaming rock, which ever flee
Upward, in glassy lines, so rapidly
We fall! From sheer excess of horror, then
(Yet still within the trance) the mental ken
Becomes a blank, until the searèd gaze,—
Blue seas, fair skies, and slanting Eastern trees
That graceful bend beneath the aromatic breeze.
Passion of Dream-life! in thy vast domain,

---

*The idea of *Amenophra*,—so far as there *is* any tangible idea attached to such a mere fragment,—was suggested to me by reading Charles Baudelaire's *La Vie Antérieure*.

†O sollecito dubbio e fredda temà / Che pensando l'accrescio.—TASSO.

Where there is much of pleasure, more of pain,
Where incorporeal Silence takes a Form,
And forests reel beneath a windless storm;[*]
Where the weird chaos of a spectral world
Leaves the dazed mind on heaps of horror hurled!—
Down thy enormous, sunless, silent isles
I late have fared. Sardonic, fearful smiles
Writhed on the stony lips of many a head
Of carven marble,—at my echoing tread
A mausoleum, towering in the gloom,
Swung wide its ponderous gates, to give me room! .
But still I journeyed on, and did emerge
at last, upon this glorious, boundless verge,
Where, gazing through the blue infinite space,
My soul identified its earlier dwelling-place.

I have long idled here, a life away
Beneath vast marble porticoes,—each day,
Bathed in cool caverns of perfumèd shade
And fanned by graceful Nubian slaves, arrayed

---

[*] And wandering amid those awful hills, I beheld sombre and moss-bearded
pine-forests, the which were of vast size and inconceivable age . . . tossing
their arms wildly to the sky, and crashing against each other, *the while there
was no breath of wind stirring beneath that gloomy and evil vault.*—TRITEMIUS.

In grotesque garbs. Only at night and morn
Could I see the marine sun's rays adorn
The rolling sea with rich prismatic fires
And gild th' Eaternal City's thousand spires,—
Save when I left the couch, the shade, the band
Of slaves, to pace the ribbed and tawny sand.
Then all the blazoned colors of the sky
Were mirrored in my own reflective eye,
And so gave me, throughout the night and day,
Strange dreams with which the while the time away.
The slaves, whose unique duty was to find
And exorcise the care that weighed my mind
With growing melancholy, danced in vain
Their graceful measures to assuage my pain.
Or, Seraph-like, evoked 'threttándo'*
From trembling strings that only voiced my woe.
For an old sage in passing by had said,
In words that seared my soul like molten lead,
"Dream, Amenophra, dream on while the breath
Of Summer fans thy cheek,—full many a death

---

*This is the beautiful representative echo by which Aristophanes expresses
the sound of the Grecian *phorminx*, or some other instrument, which
conjecturally has been shown most to resemble our modern European
harp.—DE QUINCEY.

And resurrection wait thee, ere thy soul
Shall know the great peace of the final goal."

Still in the trance, I traced my tortuous way
Back through the spectral world of solemn gray;
Still in the dream, I wandered 'neath the smiles
(Frozen and joyless mirth!) that in those isles
Leered saturnine from out the Stygian gloom,
Or mocked me from the carvings on the tomb!
But all the formless phantoms that of yore
Had triumphed o'er me with their hellish lore
I feared no longer: at the last hour of night
'Tis seen, light grows invisible through light,—
Dawn breaks, the brightest planet fades away
Before th' effulgence of the orb of day.
And so, by virtue of the deeper shade
I did not see the lesser ones which strayed
Within my ken; but still I could not flee
The face of Amenophra by the sea,
(Who was my former self!) the while he died
His glance sought mine, and almost me descried,
In proud impatience, as Death closed his eyes,
To pierce the veil, and thus his second self surmise?

[From Edkins's *Amenophra and Other Poems* (Detroit: Edwin B. Hill, 1889).]

Faces and Souls

Paul Eldridge

Faces, faces, faces . . .
An orgic dance of faces,
An insane carnival of faces . . .
Mouths and cheeks and noses,
And a crumbled Heaven of eyes,—
Eyes that shine and dim,
Like endless summer-fields
Of twinkling fireflies
Upon some moonless night—
Eyes that seek and grieve,
And laugh and weep,
And stare at last
Like oval chips
Of frozen glass . . .
Faces.
And beneath them
Souls—
Small fearing souls,
Thin, hungry souls,
Phantom sphinxes,
Obscene and cynical—
Souls yearning and sobbing,
And dying . . .
Souls that spew forever
Like slimy crustacea,

Stony masks of faces
And skulk beneath them.
Faces and souls—
In a mad dance,
In a wild carousel—
Faces and souls,
An infinite desert
Of tombs and silences . . .

[From Eldridge's *Vanitas* (Boston: Stratford Co., 1920).]

Articles

On "A Wine of Wizardry"

S. T. Joshi

One of several major omissions from August Derleth's otherwise impressive historical anthology of weird poetry, *Dark of the Moon* (1947), was the work of George Sterling. The omission was especially peculiar in light of the apparent fact that Derleth's colleague Donald Wandrei—far more attuned to poetry in general and weird poetry in particular than Derleth—was a significant behind-the-scenes advisor to the book, and he was clearly familiar with and enthusiastic about Sterling's poetry. Perhaps Derleth felt that Sterling's most notable weird poems—*The Testimony of the Suns* (1903; 644 lines) and "A Wine of Wizardry" (1907; 207 lines)—were too lengthy to include (although he seems to have had no such concerns regarding H. P. Lovecraft's sonnet cycle *Fungi from Yuggoth*, a cumulative total of 504 lines); but shorter weird poems by Sterling were readily available.

That Sterling was the mentor of the young Clark Ashton Smith was also a fact surely known to Derleth and Wandrei. Sterling in turn had been mentored by Ambrose Bierce (also omitted from *Dark of the Moon*, although there is a modicum of weird poetry amidst the mass of mostly satirical verse that he wrote over a lifetime); and one wonders whether, had he lived longer, Bierce might have come to sense that Smith ultimately outshone his master. But just as Smith gained celebrity by publishing a scintillating volume of poetry, *The Star-Treader and Other Poems* (1912), at the age of nineteen, so Sterling first came to the nation's attention when Bierce shepherded "A Wine of Wizardry" into print (in the *Cosmopolitan*, September 1907), prefaced—unusually—by a laudatory article, "A Poet and His Poem."

It is not my purpose to trace the long and convoluted history of Bierce's largely fruitless attempts to secure magazine publication of the poem from early 1904—when he first read it in manuscript—onward, nor to discuss the heated controversy the poem (and, perhaps more pertinently, Bierce's article) engendered. In part, that controversy was deliberately fostered by the Hearst papers, while from another direction Bierce's enemies—many of them stung by his own merciless dissection of their literary inadequacies—seized upon his flamboyant remarks to berate both Sterling as a flamboyant poetical novice and Bierce as an uncritical log-roller.

My chief query is much simpler: what, exactly, is the *meaning* of "A Wine of Wizardry"?

The matter is singularly difficult to ascertain. Sterling's and Bierce's remarks about the poem in their correspondence shed singularly little light on the issue. Sterling appears to have written the poem as early as late 1903 or very early 1904. In a letter of October 10, 1903, he cites the three lines from Bierce's "Geotheos"— "When mountains were stained as with wine / By the dawning of time, and as wine / Were the seas"—that he used as the epigraph to "A Wine of Wizardry," referring to them as having "indescribable beauty."[6] Then, in his letter of January 2, 1904, Sterling quotes lines 173–76 and 196–97 of the finished poem, the latter constituting the celebrated couplet "The blue-eyed vampire, sated at her feast, / Smiles bloodily against the leprous moon."[7] Late in January Sterling promised to mail Bierce his new poem. He must have done so toward the end of the month, for Bierce, in his letter to Sterling of February 5, 1904, wrote enthusiastically:

> And the poem! I hardly know how to speak of it. No poem in English of equal length has so bewildering a wealth of imagination. Not Spenser himself has flung such a profusion of pearls into so small a casket. Why,

---

6. All letters between Bierce and Sterling are in the Berg Collection of the New York Public Library.

7. George Sterling, "A Wine of Wizardry," in *Complete Poetry*, ed. S. T. Joshi and David E. Schultz (New York: Hippocampus Press, 2013), 1.77–82. Subsequent references to the poem will occur parenthetically in the text by line number.

man, it takes away the breath! I've read and reread—read it for the expression and read it for the thought (always when I speak of the "thought" in your work I mean the meaning—which is another thing) and I shall read it many times more.

In his reply (February 10, 1904), Sterling says next to nothing about the poem save to express gratitude at Bierce's favorable opinion. In a letter April 22, 1904, Sterling states that "I think I'll add a few more verses to my wine poem, and when I've done so would like to send you a new copy." Sterling did just that, although it is unclear how extensive the additions were. Bierce does mention, in a letter of April 17, 1905, that "your two new and fine lines in 'A Wine of Wizardry' are well placed where you put them"; and Sterling notes in a letter of November 19, 1905, that he has added some twenty-five lines to the poem. As late as June 10, 1907, Sterling is speaking of "new lines" to the poem, so it is evident that he continued to tinker with the poem almost up to the time of its first magazine appearance. It was in his letter of June 19, 1907, that Sterling formally asked Bierce whether he could use the three lines from "Geotheos" as the epigraph to the poem. (These were omitted from the *Cosmopolitan* publication, because Bierce felt that their appearance would cast doubt upon the sincerity or objectivity of Bierce's article about the poem.)

But Sterling himself says next to nothing about what his poem "means," or what his purpose was in writing it. To some degree he felt it a pendant to *The Testimony of the Suns*, but perhaps only in the sense that it was a long poem with vivid imagery. In a letter of February 10, 1904, he says to Bierce: "I asked you if I would better try to write in a vein similar to 'A Wine of Wizardry', poetry purely 'unhuman' and imaginative, or in the line of the 'Testimony', semi-scientific verse. I'm anxiously awaiting your decision." This is not terribly helpful, as it could be argued that *Testimony* could be considered the more "unhuman" of the two, since it is chiefly concerned with the cosmic conflicts of the stars (the second part of the poem attempts to draw parallels between these conflicts and human society, but the parallels are a trifle opaque), whereas the essence of "A Wine of Wizardry"—the wide and all but incalculable range of the imagination—seems more fundamentally human and far less overtly cosmic than *Testimony*.

Matters are not helped by Bierce's "A Poet and His Poem," which merely showers praise upon the poem and sees in it an instance of "pure poetry" (not a phrase used by Bierce, but implied in such comments as "Their author has no 'purpose, end, or care' other than the writing of poetry. His work is as devoid of motive as is the song of the skylark—it is merely poetry"[8]). And although Bierce states that "Great lines are not all that go into the making of great poetry,"[9] he goes on to quote a number of the more notable lines and draws particular attention to Sterling's felicitous use of "epithets"—i.e., the modifiers of key nouns of the poem: "They personify, ennoble, exalt, spiritualize, endow with thought and feeling, touch to action like the spear of Ithuriel."[10] Well and good; but this get us no closer to the overall thrust or intention of the poem.

Because "A Wine of Wizardry" does not tell an actual story or have a coherent "plot," as we now know to be the case with a poem that many contemporary readers likened to it—Clark Ashton Smith's *The Hashish-Eater; or, The Apocalypse of Evil* (1920)—and because Sterling himself is so cagey as to the poem's meaning, we must infer meaning and purpose by means of the text of the poem itself. Its surface "plot" is simple enough: the first-person narrator drinks a glass of wine in a "crystal cup" (3), which allows his "Fancy" (6) to commence a kind of voyage through the realms of the imagination. It becomes evident that Fancy here is simply a stand-in for the imagination. Initially, Fancy ventures into domains marked by religion, as the lines "Sifting Satanic gules athwart his brow" (19) and "O'er blue profounds mysterious whence glow / The coals of Tartarus on the moonless air" (28-29) suggest. In other words, imagination teases out the vivid imagery inherent in Christian and pagan myth. Eastern myth also comes into play, as the references to "a Syrian treasure-house" (48) and "The brows of naked Ashtaroth" (51) indicate.

But, as Bierce pointed out to a critic who failed to understand the line "Or chaunted to the Dragon in his gyre" (66), Fancy quickly proceeds to the boundless cosmos for its inspiration ("Dragon in his

---

8. Ambrose Bierce, "A Poet and His Poem" (1907), in *Collected Works of Ambrose Bierce* (1909-12; rpt. New York: Gordian Press, 1966), 10.180.

9. Ibid., 10.181.

10. Ibid., 10.185.

gyre" refers to the constellation Draco, the Serpent). More cosmic imagery follows ("Where crafty gnomes with scarlet eyes conspire / To quench Aldebaran's affronting fire" [69-70]); but it is not long before Fancy returns to earth—and the monsters spawned by countless millennia of human myth-making: "the twilight witch" (84), "silent ghouls" (86), and so on. A passage recounting a kaleidoscope of precious minerals and jewels—"moonstone-crystal" (96), "coral twigs and winy agates" (97), "Translucencies of jasper" (98), "banded onyx" (99), "vermilion breast / Of cinnabar" (99-100)—make it clear that Sterling is writing a poem that features both pure terror and exotic beauty.

Sterling now brings Fancy back to the realm of religion ("the hushed cathedral's jeweled gloom" [125]), as she

> kneels, in solemn quietude, to mark
> The suppliant day from gorgeous oriels float
> And altar-lamps immure the deathless spark . . . (127-29)

The suggestion here, I believe, is that religion itself can be used as a means of imaginative expansion, for very quickly the imagery returns to pagan myth:

> And now she knows, at agate portals bright,
> How Circe and her poisons have a home,
> Carved in one ruby that a Titan lost . . .
> As craftily she gleans her deadly dews,
> With gyving spells not Pluto's queen can use . . .
> (136-38, 143-44)

But that Sterling's Fancy is similarly attracted to the darker aspects of Christian myth is evident in a subsequent passage:

> And Satan, yawning on his brazen seat,
> Fondles a screaming thing his fiends have flayed,
> Ere Lilith come his indolence to greet,
> Who leads from Hell his whitest queens . . . (157-60)

But even this is not enough for Fancy, who "is unsatisfied, and soon / She seeks the silence of a vaster night" (165-66). Her quest for even more potent and bizarre imagery leads her to India, where "By the Ganges' flood / She sees, in her dim temple, Siva loom" (178–79). Her stay in Asia is short-lived, as she returns to the myths of Europe (Merlin [187] and Hecate [193] are cited); and it is now that those celebrated lines about the blue-eyed vampire are found. The poem ends quietly, as the first-person narrator at last reappears: "And I . . . / Gaze pensively upon the way she went, / Drink at her font, and smile as one content" (204–7).

If the most we can say about "A Wine of Wizardry" is that it is simply a riot of fantastic imagery taken from the central myths of human society, then perhaps that is enough. Bierce was guilty only of mild exaggeration when he stated that "not in a lifetime has our literature had any new thing of equal length containing so much poetry and so little else. It is as full of light and color and fire as any of the 'ardent gems' that burn and sparkle in its lines. It has all the imagination of 'Comus' and all the fancy of 'The Faerie Queene.'"[11] The absence of a recognisable "plot," and even the relative dearth of philosophical "meaning" beyond its prodigal wealth of vibrant imagery, are not drawbacks but virtues; for the single-minded "purpose" of "A Wine of Wizardry" is to suggest the inexhaustible scope of the human imagination—an imagination that has so frequently been drawn to the evocation of horror, terror, weirdness, and bizarrerie. In that sense, the poem becomes a self-fulfilling justification for the entire realm of weird literature.

---

11. Bierce, Collected Works 10.181.

Reviews

Tim Powers, Poet

John Shirley

TIM POWERS. *Poems.* Catskill, NY: Charnel House, 2016. xv, 39 pp. $150 (numbered hc), $1200 (lettered hc).

"For reasons I can't even guess at," Tim Powers tells us, "in my stories I seem generally to present the writing of poetry as being dangerous to the poets . . . Poetry does work mysteriously; it has an elusive persuasion and paradoxical depth-in-brevity that prose can seldom achieve. I think it's a result of the constraints of rhyme and meter . . . strict rhyme and meter force the writer to discard the deliberate phrases that first come to mind, and with the second or third or tenth cast, allow the subconscious to participate. And the subconscious is nothing if not mysterious."

These remarks from the introduction to this slim, gem-like volume of poetry foreshadow its mysterious tone, its evocation of existential search, its eloquent, resigned stoicism, and its understated eeriness.

Many readers know Tim Powers from his World Fantasy Award-winning novels *Last Call* and *Declare,* or such intricate tales of the weird fantastic as *The Stress of Her Regard* (title from a Clark Ashton Smith poem), *The Skies Discrowned* (title taken a line by Swinburne), *Hide Me among the Graves* (title from verse by Lizzy Siddal), or *The Anubis Gates* (which quotes poems by the imaginary William Ashbless). Fans of his work know that Powers sometimes works poetry into his fiction—poetry, significant to the story, "written by" his characters.

The first part of *Poems* collects verses by Powers *as* Tim Powers. The second and third parts comprise poems in "character"—each section written from the point of view of a certain fictional character. We could argue that any poet is writing from within a point of view, essentially a persona. But the poems of "Thomas Marrity" and "Cheyenne Fleming" are like listening to classical pieces interpreted by particular violinists;

the fictional persona brings a particular tang, a tint, to the underlying Powers vision.

Almost all these poems are sonnets, some seeming a little more Petrarchan than Shakespearean: they set up a problem or question in the first quatrain, develop it in the second, then resolve or answer it in the ending sestet. Hence one of these fourteen-line poems fits easily on a single page. Yet the exploration of theme is so resonant, the form so strong, the rhyme scheme so precise, that the effect is almost like a painting by a Dutch Master: a single snapshot-like scene, just these few people in a commonplace room, or engaged in ordinary life on a rustic lane, yet some truth of the human condition is revealed. So it is with a Powers poem.

Whether Powers is writing naturalistically or with a resonance of ghostly romanticism, the influence of late nineteenth-century/early twentieth-century poets can be felt. "The Ouija Board," a six-sonnet poem, each sonnet leading into the next, is itself a weird tale written by "Cheyenne Fleming," as per this sample:

> And did I hear from ghosts? Well, not at first.
> The "planchette" (that's the gadget that you slide)
> Is for the ghosts to move, not you. The worst
> Mistake beginners make is to decide
> The message half-way through, and–like someone
> Impatient with a stutterer—presume
> To end the sentence for him, jump the gun:
> You've blown it then, the message won't resume.
>
> Passivity's the key—but not a key
> For you to open anything they'd hide.
> It's in the "hands" of someone else and he
> (or she, or it) who has already died,
> Is now awake again—a "person" who
> Is holding now the key that unlocks *you.*

Early on in *Poems,* in the "just Powers" section, we have an oblique taste of supernatural presence in the sonnet, "Testament":

Often there's a whisper that I hear in shadowed streets,
A breath of desperation from the tall, far seeing clouds
Or gasp of outrage from a manhole cover. Something meets
Between earth and sky, in pain, and if the shifting crowds
Can sense it, their response is only in their frightened eyes.
The very breezes pick their way among the alleyways
As if afraid of something in the gray December skies . . .

The sonnet goes on to suggest that we have failed a coming Messiah, "for our hands have written us an epitaph in rust, on crumpled steel." This perception of spiritual or moral unworthiness is a recurrent theme in *Poems*, though never bluntly stated.

Powers's skeptical attitude toward reductionism and scientific positivism emerges in his sonnet "Atoms." "Behind each atom's bland and sturdy face is vacuum," Powers tells us. The sonnet concludes:

Micro or macro, never mind the size,
The principle is constant—people bind
And link, and love, imagining they'll find
Substance in nothing—but behind your eyes
The vacuum which is all there'll ever be
Calls to the emptiness inside of me.

Besides describing the spiritual dissatisfaction of finding vacuum inside an atom, Powers is interweaving another theme: the fear that the search for authentic resolution of aloneness, whether through a lover or some starkly rational philosophy, is perhaps a hopeless quest. From "Drinking Alone":

It's just another place where you don't fit.
Your wine is black with sediment. A bit
of fresh air mightn't hurt—go start the car
And drive—it doesn't matter where you are,
Just so you're moving—till the highway swings
West, and you recognize the end of things.

Skepticism of unnuanced rationality is also found in "From Flatland to Cubeland To . . .," which suggests that we "imagine how we'd look to beings nature might allow to view us from more numerous dimensions!" The remark reverberates with something akin to Lovecraftian cosmic horror—a vibrancy that we discover, much extrapolated, in Powers's under-appreciated novel of pan-dimensional horror and old Hollywood, *Medusa's Web.* "The subconscious participating . . ."

Sometimes epigrammatic, always composed in perfect sentences, *Poems* has a quality of directness, of lucidness; yet the pure pool we're gazing into is deep, and uneasily shadowed near the bottom. There, light shades seamlessly to darkness; there we glimpse not only of fearful things but, somehow, we parse an implication of something more; something numinous, and strangely luminous.

The Virtues and Drawbacks of Free Verse

Leigh Blackmore

BENJAMIN BLAKE. *Standing on the Threshold of Madness.* n.p.: Parallel Universe Publications, 2017. 158 pp. $12.99 tpb.

I am grateful for the invitation to review this collection, though in one sense I am probably not well situated to do so, for I prefer to read, and to write, formalist verse, and Benjamin Blake's work is entirely vers libre. Nevertheless, this is a collection of weird poetry (the author's second, I believe) and as such falls well within the purview of this journal. Four of the poems here have appeared previously in print; the rest are original to this collection.

Vers libre has now been with us for over a hundred years, and such great poets as Walt Whitman, Emily Dickinson, and Ezra Pound did wonders with it. In the absence of such features of formalist verse as regular meter and rhyming with forms, we may look to other techniques that are still available to the free-verse poet—alliteration, cadences, and intonations that the poet can use to make his or her poem sound the way it is conceived to be, rather than (perhaps) forcing it into the arbitrary or artificial confines of regular meter. There is a good argument for calling free verse 'non-linear' or 'non-metrical' verse in preference to 'free,' since these terms are more accurate in delineating the nature of free verse by contrast with its historically dominant cousin, the rhyming, metered poem.

There is no denying that Blake has a telling way with imagery. Focusing on surreal juxtapositions of images and atmospheres, unnatural events, time and death, dark occultism, blood, killers, and so on, many of the poems here fall hauntingly on the mind's eye.

Some of Blake's imagery is particularly memorable, as for instance in "Candleflame," where we encounter

> Inhuman eyes, hair damp and lifeless
> A skeleton draped in skin

Blake tends to be repetitious of some of his themes—there are at least four or five poems here dealing with wolves and/or werewolves—and other traditional tropes of the macabre feature fairly heavily (vampires, churches, old-fashioned villages with priests, horses, and cobblestoned streets). There is some balance in subject matter, however, for plenty of the poems feature modern devices such as cameras and modern locales such as hospitals, even if these are depicted as lonely and deserted places akin to the cemeteries that are also featured in many poems.

The poems also vary in length from several lines to a page in length, which adds some spice to the mix. However, it cannot be denied that some of the common limitations of vers libre are on display here.

In poems such as "Something Hidden," where pronouns are omitted, on reading a line such as "Fire dances in eyes of pearl" the reader is liable to wonder "in *whose* eyes?" The phrase "ensconcing woodlands" is clumsy: while "ensconcing" is the present participle of the word "ensconce," meaning "To establish oneself in a safe, or snug place," it is here used incorrectly as an adjective.

In the same poem, the last seven lines read:

> Tiny razor-sharp teeth
> Pierce a wrist

> The blood flows warm and true
> Rivulets run down her cheeks and chin
> Her lithe neck
> And between pert perfect breasts
> I lie exsanguinated.

Re: the wrist in the first and second lines above, the same criticism as for "eyes of pearl" applies—*whose* wrist? Given that in the last line the poem's narrator identifies herself or himself by using the word "I," it might have been clearer to write "Pierce *my* wrist" at line 2 above. There is an imprecision in lines 3–7 above as to whether it is the *blood* that runs between her breasts, or whether the *narrator* lies exsanguinated between her breasts, or both. This imprecision is directly attributable to the lack of punctuation, and that lack is a feature of these poems, most of which are entirely bereft of punctuation.

The absence of pronouns causes vagary in other poems, e.g. in "Burning Churches" we have the line "A gaze that impales," which occurs without context; and the reader may again ask "*whose* gaze?"

Now, the poet may be deliberately intending to create fragmentary and ambiguous images, and if so, nothing can be said against the technique. Perhaps one could argue that the technique allows for extra subtext, since the meaning is not readily and straightforwardly interpretable. Nevertheless, for my taste, such vagaries hinder rather than help.

Another instance of this occurs in "Normal Hill Cemetery" with its lines

> Cemetery stones
> Sitting beneath layers of ice and snow
> Strolling quietly alone, camera in hand
> Trying to capture something unspoken.

Punctuation was invented for a reason, and is useful in poetry as well as prose. Dispensing with it is risky. Here the reader would not be blamed for being jarred out of the poem by the idea that cemetery stones are strolling quietly alone, whereas of course this is not what the poet intends.

There are other, more troubling infelicities of language—the author's consistent use of the word "lay" or "lays" instead of "lie" or "lies," as in the title "To *Lay* with Wolves," the line "Its doors lay off their hinges" ("Atonal"), "she lays still upon the still-made bed" ("Art Collector"), and "I will take you were you lay" ("Retractable Claws; note here that 'where' is misspelt 'were'). There is a sprinkling of other typos or misspellings such as 'lightening' (for 'lightning') ("Ambulance Bay") and incorrect usages such as "renders [for 'rends'] the sky asunder" in "Before Dawn." In "Vulpes Vulpes" (a previously published poem) we have the line (surely ungrammatical in anyone's book) "the winter has set in proper." While these infelicities do little to detract from the overall impact of the powerful imagery in the collection, they do highlight the need for a keen pair of editorial eyes on the typescript.

More oddly, a few lines are completely uninterpretable. What are we to make of "A man starts of genuflect in a velvet voice" ("Reredos")?

Despite the reservations I have expressed above, Blake's work is affecting, and I am sure we will be hearing more from him. Look out for this collection; it will reward you.

Notes on Contributors

Ross Balcom lives in southern California. His poems have appeared in *Beyond Centauri, inkscrawl, Poetry Midwest, Scifaikuest, Star*Line,* and other publications. He is a frequent contributor to *Songs of Eretz Poetry Review.*

David Barker has been a fan of weird literature all his life. Recently, his writings have appeared in *Fungi, Cyäegha,* and *Shoggoth.net.* In collaboration with W. H. Pugmire, David has had two books published by Dark Renaissance Books: *The Revenant of Rebecca Pascal* (2014) and *In the Gulfs of Dream and Other Lovecraftian Tales* (2015).

F. J. Bergmann manifests in *Analog, Asimov's Science Fiction, Apex,* and elsewhere in the alphabet, and functions, so to speak, as poetry editor of *Mobius: The Journal of Social Change* and in other literary roles. *A Catalogue of the Further Suns* (dystopian first-contact poems), the Gold Line Press chapbook contest winner, appears in 2017.

Leigh Blackmore has written weird verse since age thirteen. He has lived in the Illawarra, New South Wales, Australia, for the last decade. He has edited *Terror Australis: Best Australian Horror* (1993) and *Midnight Echo 5* (2011) and written *Spores from Sharnoth & Other Madnesses* (2008). A nominee for SFPA's Rhysling Award (Best Long Poem), Leigh is also a four-time Ditmar Award nominee. He is currently assembling an edition of *The Selected Letters of Robert Bloch.*

Adam Bolivar, a native of Boston, now residing in Portland, Oregon, has had his weird fiction and poetry appear in the pages of *Nameless,* the *Lovecraft eZine, Spectral Realms,* and Chaosium's *Steampunk Cthulhu* and *Atomic Age Cthulhu* anthologies. His first book, *The Fall of the House of Drake,* was published by Dunhams Manor Press in 2015.

Sunni K Brock's fiction and poetry combines science fiction, horror, fantasy, and erotica. As one-half of the team of JaSunni Productions, LLC and Cycatrix Press, she creates genre film and print with her husband,

Jason. If she had spare time, she would pursue genealogy, shopping at the farmer's market, and conducting experiments on controlled randomness.

G. O. Clark's writing has been published in *Asimov's Science Fiction, Analog, Space & Time, A Sea of Alone: Poems for Alfred Hitchcock, Tales of the Talisman, Daily SF, Jupiter(GB),* and elsewhere. He is the author of eleven poetry collections, most recently *Built to Serve: Robot Poems* (2017). His fiction collection *Twists & Turns* (Alban Lake Publishing) came out in 2016. He was a Stoker Award finalist in poetry, 2011. He lives in Davis, California.

Frank Coffman is professor of English, journalism, and creative writing at Rock Valley College in Rockford, Illinois. His primary interests as a critic are in the rise and relevance of popular imaginative literature across the genres of adventures, detection and mystery, fantasy, horror and the supernatural, and science fiction. He has published several articles on these genres and is the editor of Robert E. Howard's *Selected Poems.*

Deborah L. Davitt was raised in Reno, Nevada, but received her M.A. in English from Penn State. She currently lives in Houston with her husband and son. Her poetry has garnered two Rhysling nominations and has appeared in nearly twenty journals; her short fiction has appeared in *InterGalactic Medicine Show, Compelling Science Fiction, Altered Europa,* and *Silver Blade.* Her well-received Edda-Earth series is available through Amazon.

Ashley Dioses is a writer of dark fiction and poetry from Southern California. Her poetry has appeared in *Weird Fiction Review, Spectral Realms, Xnoybis, Weirdbook, Gothic Blue Book,* Volume 5 (Burial Day Books, 2015), and elsewhere. She is working on her first book of weird poetry.

Poems by **Kendall Evans** have appeared in *Weird Tales, Analog, Asimov's,* and other magazines. His stories have appeared in *Amazing, Weirdbook, Fantastic,* and elsewhere. His novel *The Rings of Ganymede,* a ring cycle in the tradition of Wagner's operas and Tolkien's *Lord of the Rings,* is now available (Alban Lake Books, 2014).

Ian Futter began writing stories and poems in his childhood, but only lately has started to share them. One of his poems appears in Jason V Brock's anthology *The Darke Phantastique* (Cycatrix Press, 2014), and he continues to produce dark fiction for admirers of the surreal.

Liam Garriock is an author and poet who counts authors such as Kafka, Arthur Machen, J. G. Ballard, Lovecraft, William S. Burroughs, Borges, Poe, William Blake, and Philip K. Dick as among his many touchstones. He lives in Edinburgh, Scotland.

Maxwell I. Gold is a native of Columbus, Ohio, and began his interests in creative writing at a young age. He studied philosophy at the University of Toledo then began seriously pursuing his interests in a career of writing and composition after college. His focuses are on supernatural horror literature, fantasy, as well as literary fiction, short stories, and prose-poetry.

Chad Hensley is a Bram Stoker Award–nominated author who had his first book of poetry, *Embrace the Hideous Immaculate,* published in May 2014 from Raw Dog Screaming Press. His recent poetry appearances include *Skelos* #2 and #3, the *Horror Writers Association Horror Poetry Showcase* III and IV, *The Audient Void* #2 and #3, *Weirdbook* #32 and #33, and the previous six issues of *Spectral Realms*.

S. T. Joshi has edited the poetical works of Clark Ashton Smith (2007–8), Donald Wandrei (2008), H. L. Mencken (2009), H. P. Lovecraft (2013), and George Sterling (2013), all for Hippocampus Press. His brief treatise *Emperors of Dreams: Some Notes on Weird Poetry* was published in 2008 by P'rea Press. He has written many critical and biographical studies in the realm of weird fiction.

Charles D. O'Connor III is a thirty-three-year-old prose poet of the strange residing in Virginia. This issue of *Spectral Realms* marks his second appearance and his fifth prose piece published overall. He is making his mark slowly but surely. The poem appearing here he dedicates, first, to his late father Charles O'Connor Jr., dear late friend Dr. William C. Farmer, and his ancestor Dr. Robert Thornton, famous botanist.

K. A. Opperman is a poet with a predilection for the strange, the Gothic, and the grotesque, continuing the macabre and fantastical tradition of such luminaries as Poe, Clark Ashton Smith, and H. P. Lovecraft. His first verse collection, *The Crimson Tome,* was published by Hippocampus Press in 2015.

Manuel Pérez-Campos is currently preparing a collection of his poetry in addition to a collection of essays on H. P. Lovecraft. His literary research has been published in *Lovecraft Annual* #4; his poetry has appeared in *Spectral Realms* #6 and is also forthcoming in *Weird Fiction Review* #8. His professional background is in psychotherapy. Born in Santiago, Cuba, of Lebanese-Spanish descent, he now lives in Bayamón, Puerto Rico.

A native of northwest Indiana, **Nathaniel Reed**'s work heavily reflects and draws from this locale, often borrowing settings from the dunes and marshes surrounding Lake Michigan. He currently studies biology and education at Purdue Northwest and will soon be graduating and beginning his career as a high school teacher. He thanks Whitney Wilmoth for her early readings and encouragement.

A couple recent books by **Jessica Amanda Salmonson** include *The Weird Epistles of Penelope Pettiweather, Ghost Hunter* (Alchemy Press), *The Death Sonnets* (Rainfall), and *Pets Given in Evidence of Old English Witchcraft and Other Bewitched Beings* (Sidecar Preservation Society). She has recently contributed novelettes, short stories, and poems to *Weird Tales, Weirdbook, The Audient Void, Space & Time, Skelos,* etc. Her Ace Books trilogy *The Tomoe Gozen Saga* has recently come back into print from Open Road Media as audiobooks and ebooks.

Ann K. Schwader lives and writes in Colorado. Her most recent collections are *Dark Energies* (P'rea Press, 2015) and *Twisted in Dream* (Hippocampus Press, 2011). Her *Wild Hunt of the Stars* (Sam's Dot, 2010) and *Dark Energies* were Bram Stoker Award finalists. She is also a two-time Rhysling Award winner (2010 and 2015) and was the Poet Laureate for NecronomiCon Providence 2015.

John Shirley is the author of numerous novels and books of short stories. His latest novel is *Doyle After Death* (HarperCollins, 2013), a tale of Sir Arthur Conan Doyle in the afterlife. He won the Bram Stoker Award for his story collection *Black Butterflies*.

Claire Smith's poems have previously appeared in *Spectral Realms* as well as the other journals *Illumen* and *Trysts of Fate*. She has also been published in the anthologies *The Night Café* (Alban Lake Publishing,

2016) and *Fossil Lake II: The Re-fossiling* (Sabledrake Enterprises, 2015). She holds an M.A. in English (Open University). She currently lives in Gloucestershire, England.

Christina Sng is a poet, writer, and artist. Her work has appeared in numerous venues worldwide and garnered nominations in the Dwarf Stars and Rhysling Awards, as well as honorable mentions in *The Year's Best Fantasy and Horror*. She is the author of *A Collection of Nightmares, Astropoetry*, and Elgin nominee *An Assortment of Sky Things*.

Ronald Terry earned a B.A. and M.A. in English from the University of Southern Mississippi, where he wrote his M.A. thesis on the poetry of Ted Hughes. He published his first poem in 1980; since then his poems have appeared in many print and online publications such as *Poetrybay, Dead Snakes, Night Cry, Space and Time, The Horror Zine, Star*Line*, among others.

Richard L. Tierney's *Collected Poems* appeared from Arkham House in 1981. A later volume of poetry was published as *Savage Menace and Other Poems of Horror* (P'rea Press, 2010). Tierney is also the author of *The Winds of Zarr* (Silver Scarab Press, 1975), *The House of the Toad* (Fedogan & Bremer, 1993), and many other works of horror and fantasy fiction.

Born on Walpurgisnacht, **Don Webb** has had an affinity for the mysterious as shown in his books on topics such as Aleister Crowley or the Greek Magical Papyri. A Rhysling nominee, his first full-length poetry collection is due in some months from Dynatox Ministries. Three of his poems have made it into dark rock and roll.

M. F. Webb was raised in the desert Southwest and now makes her home in a Victorian seaport town in the Pacific Northwest, where she is finalizing her historical fantasy novel about Captain Jas. Hook. Her poetry has appeared in previous issues of *Spectral Realms* and her fiction in *Latchkey Tales*.

Mary Krawczak Wilson has written poetry, fiction, plays, articles, and essays. She was born in St. Paul, Minnesota, and moved to Seattle in 1991. Her most recent essay appeared in the *American Rationalist*.